The Deutsche Nationalbibliothek lists this publication in the Deutsche Nationalbibliografie; detailed bibliographic data are available in the Internet at http://dnb.d-nb.de.

vice versa, Potsdam

Cover Design: Elise Werner, Potsdam
Layout: Désiré Arnold, Berlin
Manufactured and published by:
Books on Demand, Norderstedt, Germany
Printed in Germany, 2010
ISBN 978-38423 3104-4
1st edition, 2010

First Drafts II

edited by
Désiré Arnold
and
Elise Werner

First Drafts II

A Project- creative writing: composed in a class room, composed on a meadow, composed by students of the University of Potsdam, composed by ambitious and courageous writers, composed in language, composed in a second language, composed in a third language.
A Project- A Composition.

Désiré Arnold and Elise Werner (ed.)

August 2010

Thanks for "creative input" to Gary Lovan, our instructor in the course "Creative Writing" at the University Potsdam.

Thanks for financial support to the Fachschaftsrat Anglistik/ Amerikanistik at the University of Potsdam.

Elise Werner   11

    Tuesday Night   13

    Silenced Worship   19

    The Chesire Cat's Vision   23

    City Rally - Mass Psychosis   29

    The Bedroom Window   37

Eszter Molnár   41

    Timeless Tea Time   43

    Live Slow Die Old   49

    The Impossible Potatoe Salad   66

    If Policemen Had Heartaches   69

Désiré Arnold   71

    So Sensual   73

    Nearby a River   75

    Erotic Things   77

    If   79

    Prelude to Macbeth   81

    A Different Perspective   89

Josta van Bockxmeer   101

      Anna Blume Eats a Lot   103

      Woordeloos   113

      Sprachverwirrung   115

Regine Glaß   117

      Lisa   119

      The Prayer   121

      Turned into Sitcom Dialog   125

      Girl Disguised as a Squirrel   127

      Things and -Ships   129

      Wood   135

Marcus Rehm   139

      A Brother's Confession   141

Elise Werner

Tuesday Night[1]

Tuesday night, 3 am. I get off my bike, fasten it to the fence, then drag myself up the stairs. Searching for the right key for a minute or so, I finally open the door, then go straight to bed, somehow managing to switch on the alarm.

Hardly fallen asleep, I awake from some ear-splitting racket. With an effort I stretch out my arm and switch off the alarm. Half past six. I lie down again, thinking that I won't be able to eat anything anyway, just have a coffee...

At 7 am I hastily get up. It is 30 minutes to the university, and the course starts at 7.30. I randomly throw some stuff into my bag, rush to the bathroom, then down the stairs, cursing when unlocking my bike. I cycle down the roads as fast as I can. The lights of my bike don't work, damn it. About 15 minutes later, thinking of coffee and anticipating the end of the course, I hear a muffled voice from behind. Turning around, I recognize a bike close behind me. The cyclist is just switching off his mobile. I speed up a little, then

---

1   Inspired by a story told by Veronica Bove

turn my head discretely. The bike is as close to me as before.

Suddenly a police van drives in from the left, blocking the road before me. Six policemen get out of the car, as I start wondering what this is all about. I remember that I cycle through the dark without lights, but reason that there must be some other problem. Perhaps they have searched for the man behind me. However the men and women greet each other with a slight bob of their heads, then face me.

"Your I.D., please!", they command. Feeling really uncomfortable now, I realize that I left my purse at home. A red-faced policeman steps forward.

"Get into the van.", he says aggressively.

"What?" I answer, and my uneasiness turns into fear.

"You know it, so don't waste our time. Get into the van now." he repeats, glaring at me.

Some minutes later, we enter a police station, where I am led into a small cell.

"Wait here.", they command.

I start to understand that I am being accused of something. Actually, I am already judged guilty, as long as I can't prove my innocence. I just wonder about the nature of the crime I am supposed to be tangled up in. They give me a lot of time to think about it. About an hour later, I start to panic. Trying to calm myself, I search for possible explanations.

Two hours later or so, the red-faced policeman comes in. He stands up straight before me, considering me for a while, then puts his hands on the table, still gazing at me.

"What is he planning", he starts his interrogation.

"Who are you talking about?" I wouldn't want him to think that I was afraid, and fortunately, I am getting angry now. His behavior makes me aggressive.

"Don't be stupid. We will get it out of you anyway." Holding up my mobile in front of me, he adds: "He will call sooner or later, and then you speak to him. You tell him to meet you somewhere as soon as possible, and then we come along, and arrest him."

"Well, if you think so", I answer coolly. I wonder how long I will have to wait for this call. Then suddenly, my cellphone rings.

"There!" says the policeman confidently. "Maybe it's him. No mistakes now! Do as I told you!" He hands over the phone, and I take the call, nearly laughing when seeing the word "MUM" on the screen.

"Hello?"

"Hi dear, how are you? I thought you might come around for dinner tonight?"

"Hi Mum, well, I will come if I can. But first I need you to get me out of the police station. I forgot my I.D., and apparently they've confused me with someone else. They are interrogating me. So could you please drive over to my apartment, fetch my I.D., and then come here?"

The policeman looks at me suspiciously.

"Give me the phone!" I hand it over before he can snatch it out of my hand.

"Who is speaking?" He asks unpleasantly. I hear my mother say her name, then asking what is going on.

"That's what we have to find out.", the policeman answers, awkwardly now. "Just come over here." He tells her the address.

About 30 minutes later, my mum arrives. Some more policemen and -women exchange awkward looks when they check the I.D. Then they finally let me go. I tell them that I really don't appreciate their methods, but they just answer that it was a matter of utmost importance. Or at least that's what they thought it to be. Maybe they mistook me for the wife of a mafia boss or something, they wouldn't tell me.

Silenced Worship (Mute Encounter)

"Alright", I say, "I will accompany you." We get into the car, me driving, and my mother sitting next to me. Some time later, we enter the city. I look around for a parking lot, regretting that I can't just go for a walk. When we get out of the car, I pick up a matchbox, after nearly having stepped onto it. "Aquarisbar" is written on it. I pocket it, then we walk down the road, cross a kind of market place, and enter the church. Walking down the corridor between the rows, I have a look-around. It is a huge and very impressive church, a cathedral, I should say. We walk into a row in the middle of the building, and I sit down next to a girl with very short brown hair, and a pearl-necklace. I greet her, while my mother takes the seat to my right. Waiting for the priest to start his preach, I consider the ceiling. I'm sitting right underneath the domed roof. I'm studying the paintings, golden statues and ornaments for a while, then, hearing the priest greeting the church attenders, I lower my eyes to the front. I attempt to listen, but give it up soon, starting to wonder about the girl next to me instead. Making a side glance to the right, I see my mother listen intensely, then try to look discreetly over to the girl. Of course she recognizes it. She actually is watching me, seemingly not too interested in the sermon. Looking down to the floor rapidly, I try to fgure out a possibility to communicate with her. Speaking is impossible with the people around us being incredibly silent. My eyes still on the floor, I wonder what she is doing here. A small plastic bag is lying underneath the seat in front of me. Putting my foot onto it, I drag it back as to read the writing on it. "KIDDY BEAR" is wrtten on the top, with a would-be-cute drawing of a bear underneath. Apparently, the bear has two names, as on the bottom of the bag it reads "Kitty Bear". I feel the urge to pick up the bag as to consider it more closely, but still feeling the girl's eyes on me, I refrain from it. I then remember the matches. Aquarisbar. I take them out and check the address written on its side. It is the same city. Slowly, as not to alarm my mother by a sudden movement, I search my jacket for some kind of pen, but can't find any. Looking over to the girl, I make a short gesture as if writing, then look to the front of the church. The girl hands over a pencil. With another side-glance at my mother, I write "Fr, 8 p.m." onto the matchbox, then pass it to the girl. I don't dare looking over to her again, while she reads the short message. She searches her pockets. I then receive a small yellow stone in exchange for the matches. It is Citrin. Half an hour later, with the mess finished, my mother stands up to leave. She advances a few steps, then turns and waits for me. My mother starts talking to me, something about "daughter and mother", and "nice", and "like we used to" and "should do it more often". I get up slowly. I say goodbye to the girl, then turn and walk out of the church.

The Cheshire Cat's Vision of Wonderland

Guess who's the true master of wonderland: yes, naturally, it's me, the Cheshire cat. Why else would I be grinning all the time? My sphere of control is as wide as my grin. It might sound pretentious, and it would be, if it wasn't true.

Now with the current state of affairs I have to get rid of our monarch, the Red Queen. The most difficult step is done: I have convinced the extremely peaceful, sweet-tempered, dull-witted, um, White Queen sufficiently of the evil character of her sister, and so she agreed to getting rid of her. Of course I wanted to have her sentenced to death, as she is always so eager herself to behead everyone, but well, the White Queen only wants to ban her... Anyway, we, I mean, I ordered this foolish White Rabbit to make a trip to the humans' world as to fetch this girl who once came here by accident, tumbling into the rabbit hole, in her early childhood. She seems to be ... well, she is predestined to fight the champion of the Red Queen. And she will win the battle. It might be helpful to convince her of it, for actually she rather desires to leave this place as soon as possible, as she did last time. Anyway she won't be able to resist the White Queen, so there should be no problems here... Well, here comes my friend, the Mad Hatter, bringing her along.

Hello, Alice, come here, I'm to guide you to the, um, admirable White Queen, well, she might tell you how to get out of here. Of course it is a pity that you want to leave us already, considering all the effort you made, the trouble you had to go through to get here.

The girl is looking at me suspiciously, but I'm prepared. I can easily read her thoughts. Well, I have to admit that I do not possess the power to do so by myself, but as I am able to command all creatures in wonderland, I will ask a company of mind readers to help me out. Yes, those incredibly small beings are able to enter the head of a person, read thoughts, then re-inscribe them into another person' brain, so that the latter thinks them as though they were his own thoughts. Anyway, those mind readers are so incredibly small that they don't have to enter the head through the ears or such nonsense but can take the shortcut through skin and skull. Of course "reading thoughts"

24

seems to be a metaphorical expression, however, thoughts actually are engraved into the many windings and plaitings of the brain, and as there is such an amount of thoughts, they are written so small that no one else but the incredibly small mind readers would ever be able to read them. This is also the reason for higher developed creatures having a brain much more complex than, for example, a sparrow which is only good for serving me as dinner... Also the incredibly small mind readers are the only ones to know where to find which kind of thoughts, and how to sort them out, and put them into a comprehensible structure. Well, that only by the way.

The team I engaged is just coming back from Alice's head and has entered mine. The negative side-effect is that I can't prevent them from reading my own precious thoughts and genius ideas. I recognize their arrival in my head by starting to think disagreeable things about myself. Well, this silly Alice-girl is rather amusing me by thinking of me as a "lazy cat" sporting an enormous grin. She thinks of false friendliness and actually is imagining my teeth, which are still clenched together in a "terrible grin", opening widely in a minute or so, clearing the view onto sharp edges, then moving forward with sudden vitality, swallowing the poor girl entirely with one bite. "What a foolish land" Alice concludes wisely, "such a telltale amount of color – gives away the whole hypocrisy of the place. It is just a big trap. Or a small one, seeing how much I had to diminish my size to get in here, but a complex one anyway".

"Well" says Alice "I wonder why this rabbit was in such a hurry. And why making me come here? I hope someone will finally tell me?"

Grinning even wider, I say "the Queen is going to enlighten you on this business, I mean, on your business here". With the Red Queen disabled, it will be no big deal to control the White Queen, so that finally I will rule the whole realm: I am going to be the true Queen of Wonderland without anyone recognizing it. Obviously, as I might have mentioned, I am the most powerful and capable creature here, so it is only natural that it must be me who rules the place. But as leaders are easily attacked or disliked, I'm not even thinking of ruling openly. More gloriously I will rule in secret. People can't even imagine the amount of extra-power this political trick is going to earn me.

All well so far. Alice greets the White Queen with a sound of admiration. The Queen just could not fail to charm the girl, to convince her to fight the Red Queen's champion, this stupid Jabber-something dragon who is just big and heavy, and flies around spitting fire, but that's about it.

The White Queen is already making friends with Alice, telling her our plan to throw down the Red Queen's cruel ruler-ship. Hearing a number of "We need your help"s and "You can do your part in making this realm become a better place"s, I think it is the right time to leave for the Red Queen, in the role of the White Queen's messenger of course, and inform her that the champion has arrived, and that the battle is to take place in the evening to follow.

No human reign is fit for the wants of cats and other animals. Still much more of them than humans live in wonderland. My reign is to bring justice. Democracy...

There we go, the battle has started. I have a good view on the armed Alice. The champions greet each other... well, actually they don't, who cares, their business is killing the opponent before... you know how it works. So ... oh, this was a nice stroke, I mean, strike! Be aware Alice! She won't fail... There it is, nice clear cut through the throat! Well I thank you, Alice, I will even lead you back to the gate of your own place. There, everything is fine now. I really owe you my thanks, Alice, in the name of the White Queen, who is the good Queen... and in the name of all cats, I mean, good creatures of wonderland.

City Rally – Mass Psychosis

Down the stairs. 12th floor, 11th floor, 10th floor, 9th floor. A woman presses the button for the lift. I hear the rumbling sounds of the lift moving: 8th floor, 7th floor, 6th floor, 5th floor. A young woman with a big yellow dog enters the lift, while the woman of the 9th floor leaves it, then, recognizing that she has not arrived at the bottom yet, re-enters. 4th floor, 3rd floor, 2nd floor, 1st floor. People transporting an enormous cupboard wait in front of the lift. Ground floor. Two women and a dog leave the lift. I take the last steps down and leave the building to the front door. I unlock my bike. I hasten to the train station. I search for a free parking lot and fasten my bike to the metal stake. I reconsider. I unlock my bike and take it along, into the station, then down the crowded moving stairs. People stand   paralyzed.

In the priority-for-bikes-and-wheelchairs-and-buggies-compartment all seats are taken. Putting my bike in front of the people earns me reproachful glares. Holding onto my bike, I take out my book, longing for a coffee. Someone storms into the compartment to my left, then leaves it to my right. People shake their heads.

29

I read: "… are we supposed to dare to enter the inner parts of our misconception and self-recognition, just go, together, one after the other, the sound of breaking walls in our ear".

I struggle out of the train half an hour later, others squeeze into it. On the platform, people run around. Like ants, following their business, making the whole thing work. They receive their share, but no one understands the complexity of the interaction. Not even the queen. I take the lift. I descend two floors. I go up again, this time taking the stairs. Next to me the moving stairs that make people fall into some trance, not hurrying anymore. The moving stairs hurry for them.

Out of the station. Busy ants running, cycling, driving, very skilled. Trains like maggots round up the image. Me cycling along, checking my appearance in a window as I pass by. Stores become replaced by dwelling houses. I cross a bridge. A river branch forms a kind of lake underneath. Complex life goes on down there, too, but I only see the smooth surface of the water. Only a few little waves. Ships make the river metamorphose into a road. Unaware of the society underneath. Under water, but not yet drowned.

I enter a building. Time drags on, but never stands still. I leave the building, unlock my bike, return the way I came. Near the first super-market, a guy greets me, makes me stop, then asks for money. We went to school together, so I hand over a one euro coin. Ask him how he is doing. He tells about the social welfare office apparently being shut down, and about his shoes and that he is in need of water-proof socks. I tell him I might buy him second-hand military boots. But I think he does not believe me. I say goodbye and leave him behind. It has been worse, I think ... but how should I know and what does it mean to me? To anyone? It started with him telling me of quietly whispering voices nibbling at him, with half-grown monsters... I remember him telling me: I might go to the house of tea/ maybe there are noodles in a threesome/ I see something that you do not see/ I drive to the therapy with utmost fun /You then encounter a true psychologist /with all the nurses staring at me/ Sizzling noises, hardly audible, in between...

Shaking off those memories, I enter the station, then another train. A man is bubbling. He comes closer. I hear him say: Someone...mm...tellthetruth! People shaking heads. Others kissing. Reading. Listening to music. I read only one sentence, "...they have made of each of us the one they needed us to be...", then I have to get off the train.

Like on command, about half of the people on the crowded platform fall to the floor, then stretch their arms upwards, saying something about the need of resurrection. Shocked first, I remember the flash-mob trend: people meet in a public place, and perform something they agreed upon beforehand on the internet, at a precise time and place. The people around look troubled only for a second or two, then some shake their heads, and follow their business. The flash-mob, too, stands up, its members stray into different directions, leaving me wondering about resurrection, and arranged mass-psychosis. And how it might belong together. Is not the latter the precondition for the former?

Bicycling for a minute or so, I sit down on a meadow. I will meet someone in about ten minutes. I take out my book: "... I don't know why she asked then, whether there were human sacrifices in our land ... Of course not, I said indignantly, but she cocked her head and looked at me intriguingly. No? She said. Not even if the worst comes to the worst? I still answered no, and she said thoughtfully: Well, maybe it is true. And now, after such a long time, she has not forgotten our conversation, earlier she asked: No human sacrifices, do you still believe that? Oh, my poor friend".

A girl next to me takes off her shoes, then forces her feet into another pair. Only this pair of shoes is not visible for me. I watch her tie invisible laces in mid-air over her naked feet, and I am awestruck.She then walks around, the shoes apparently fitting well enough. She is the one I wanted to meet.

She changes back to her own pair of shoes, handing the invisible pair over to her companion. Then she goes away, and, stuffing my book into my bag, I follow her. We are supposed to meet each other in about five minutes at the well, she has not seen me yet. She sits down on the ridge of the well. I walk over, greet her, and sit down. I tell her about the human sacrifices. And we agree that they are made in harsh times, and in others. We look around, searching for someone fit for the role of being sacrificed. It might be those who are as distinguished from others as possible. Because we need to recognize them. Or else we would become aware that we have to integrate, or else we will disintegrate. She says, the whole crazy ... whatever ... blames its madness on carefully chosen individuals. Makes them believe in their own madness. I say, somehow they are integrated. Turned into pillows, stabilizing. The obvious exception from the rule. By their bare existence, they already question images and thoughts we feel so comfortable with.

I start reading from my book to my friend. It is Medea speaking: "...Either I am out of my mind, or this city is built upon a crime.... The one who gives away this secret is lost". Turned into a murderer by Euripides and Seneca, but in earlier stories she was the scapegoat. Now Medea reappears, resurrected and again different, admired, and feared, and hated. Either I am out of my mind, or this city is built upon a crime. Defamed and banished as the evil, savage woman, because she knew too much. She was just perfect to blame the guilt of a whole city upon....

I re-enter my house at night, take the lift and press the button number thirteen. I have come back to my anthill.

I have my place. It rather resembles a beehive, though, except the 200 inhabitants live in square holes instead of hexagonal ones. In fact, it is only a small part of a gigantic bee colony. Working together for something... Or within something. All busy. Or else making people be busy with them. Playing a role, anyway, as I do.

The next day I spend in a Sunday-lethargy. Sleeping, eating, reading.

Citations from Christa Wolf: Medea. Stimmen. München: Deutscher Taschenbuch Verlag, 2003. Translated by E.W. 1st citation from prologue; 2nd from p. 52; 3rd from p. 58; 4th from p.14 and 23.

37

Eszter Molnár

Timeless Tea Time or The Future Garden

A woman was sitting on the parapet of the bridge. Beneath her the lazy river was carrying boat-loads of sunbathing, half-naked girls. The boats were captained by important-looking guys, who, in spite of their boxer-shorts, managed to radiate an air of complete control which extended itself over the present into whatever future might come. The river also carried birds, ducks, swans, and crakes that, in their turn, carried their offspring on their backs, always guiding them towards safety and the autonomy of adulthood.

The woman on the bridge was wearing a wide-brimmed straw hat. Her long blond hair was streaming in the warm summer wind. Her enchanting empire-dress was playfully caressing her figure. In front of her, on the pavement, stood a fragile, iron-wrought table, faced by a matching chair. The table was covered with a white tablecloth made of intricately woven lace. There was a nicely arranged, but single, tea-set laid out on the table. The dishes were made out of the thinnest porcelain; the light could be seen shining through them. A colourful bouquet of summer flowers rounded out this impressionistic still life image of a soon to be enjoyed five-o-clock tea. Above this arrangement an old-fashioned but exquisite parasol was spanned as a protection against the furiously burning afternoon sun.

The lady was sitting gracefully on a red-velvet cushion she had previously placed on the broad and comfortable stone-parapet. She was carelessly dangling her fine legs, which could be glimpsed when the breeze from down the river became harder. Then she also had to hold on to her hat, which she playfully did, reaching up with her lace-gloved hand, carefully preventing the hat from flying into the permanent stream of cars passing over the bridge. Passing and standing; standing and passing. Rush-hour in the city.

The lady seemed oblivious to the commotion surrounding her. She did not heed the cars and she occasionally bestowed a precious smile on a passer-by. But mostly she could be seen enjoying the splendid view. From her elevated position she could see far away. She could see the fountain sprouting out of the river in front of the castle, built in the Breton style, surrounded by the tall trees of the English Garden. On the opposite side of the river the most exclusive district of the city was stretched. Behind every bourgeoisie city villa a well-kept lawn ran towards the river-bank. From there, walking over wooden-piers, the owners could reach their yachts, anchored there as a matter of course. Further on she could see the river broadening into a lake. On it, the taut sails of the sailing-boats looked like wings of a dove.

These far away pictures held her attention for a while, but the lady was also watching the scenes that presented themselves nearer to the bridge, to her high seat. On the right river bank was one of the most cherished oddities of the city: an old lido. From the wooden cabins the faded painting was slowly crumbling, but this could hardly be seen from so far away, and it surely did not bother the kids who were playing in the shallow waters. In gaudy swimming suits they were plunging into the water. Sometimes a cheerful scream pierced through the monotonous hum of the cars passing by. The splashes could not be heard from so high above.

On the left hand side the modernist building of the New Theatre loomed over the water, looking like a luxurious three-story bird nest. With its crying-red roof it was the newest venture of the city, the establishment's pride echoing from its walls. Stone steps, arranged like terraces, led to the river on this side. Cafés and restaurants beckoned to the common people who were earnestly enjoying their after-work-hours. Later on, when it became dark, the red, blue, yellow and green lights were be switched on. Their light broke into dancing little pieces on the never resting mirror of the river. There was slow, soft music; couples embraced and swayed in unison with the waves.

But first the other ones had to leave. Those who had spent their day drinking beer under the cool shade of the bridge, heedless of the future. They had collected the empty bottles, their income of a day, and stumbled homewards, following the river in the opposite direction. The slow current guided them to their temporarily fixed abodes, where they crawled under rejected linens and were buzzed them to sleep. From there they will eventually be washed away by a future flood, leaving behind the city, finally clean and neat.

After the last couple kissed their way by, the lady first collected the gilded little casket, which till then had so seamlessly hidden itself between the delicate dishes on the petite-table. In this casket a handwritten card was inserted:

> Please give
> for a good purpose!

On the other side of the card, which only the lady could see from her throne on the bridge, was written in the same hand:

> You are a beggar too.

In the little box was her day's revenue. She crossed the street onto the isle that was between the lanes and where, under a lamppost, her wooden handcart, refined with age, was parked. She carefully dragged it back across the street. Dancing to her own, inner melody she began to pile her equipment on the cart. She turned towards the heart of the city and began her descent, humming a waltz along the warmly lit streets. She found a place where she could cautiously undress and cast the tired melancholy from her soul while slowly drifting into sleep. Her dreams were filled with the various melodies of the day. The movie she sees was her property alone.

Now and then a passenger would ask the lady on the bridge what good purpose she was collecting for. She would turn her face in a friendly manner towards the questioner. Her river-green eyes would openly look into the curious one's face. With a distinguished accent uttered in a pleasant voice she would share this secret and answer thus:

"I really enjoy sitting here amongst you but I'd much rather do it in my own place."

It was a perfect day to lose my virginity. To be honest the losing itself was pretty unspectacular, but the weather and other circumstances were favourable indeed. Maybe I should not have waited for so long. I suppose nowadays 39 is considered to be a rather advanced age for defloration but I had my reasons for putting it off.

First of all I am strongly opposed to the fast-paced, high speed relationships my fellow men and women tend to involve themselves in. Not that I do not understand the urge they are following; the loud and unmistakable call of nature sounds in our every ear. But come on, we all are civilized human beings who should be able to restrain ourselves at least for culture's sake. All this sexual intercourse practised for myriads of reasons: as, or instead of, an introduction; to deepen; to tighten; to loosen; to save; or to end a relationship; out of pity, com/passion; self-assertion and -destruction; for educational, recreational, reproductive, ritual and religious reasons; and most of the time out of the oversimplified conviction of the participants that they do it out of love... They refuse to accept that love is the mixture of the above reasons in various proportions and not one consistent, well what? Thingy. A complex illusion created to mask the overestimated need for reproduction. Especially in our longitudes. Or aren't enough children born in China?

Of course these might seem to be pretty far-fetched reasons for preserving one's (my) virginity for so long. The most common assumption would supposedly be that I am too ugly, too fat, and that I am too unattractive overall to ever come near to seducing an alpha-male, or at least some overweight, semi-retired accountant, twenty years out of sexual practice. In fact, I was frequently confronted with similar notions, uttered from what others call friends. Yet another concept that is generally super-valued. Friendship, in my opinion, is just another Pavlov effect. You hear the bell, see the lemon and disgrace yourself by an uncontrollable stream of saliva running down your chin. I instantly got into that drooled state every time a friend readily signaled that s/he needed my help. And because old Pavlov was so right, I most reliably sprouted out all the sentences that were clearly meant for consolidation, assurance, and a general show of good feeling. But in the end I never got to say what I wanted to, never got to the point where I could have reviled my own, inner self. Anyway, now I know that a friend never is interested in seeing, knowing, experiencing the other, the counterpart, the you in the common we. Should have listened to Nietzsche earlier. But you live, you learn.

Do not get me wrong, I do not want to generalize and say that my experience holds true for everyone; but please do understand that as the center of my universe I can only rely on myself as a source for ultimate knowledge. If your opinions are different, I will surely not belittle you; I will just refuse to acknowledge the truth of what you are saying.

Coming back to my virginity or ultimately the loss of it, there are of course other, more personal reasons for my prolonged state of untouchedness. (I mean besides my refusal to believe in love and friendship as constituting entities of social intercourse, which in itself, of course, might be seen as a barrier between me and any opportunity to exchange body fluids.) As a person, who refuses to live by the rules society so kindly enforces upon one, I see myself as a criminal, an offender against everything that is assumed. And like any criminal, I beg mercy for my crimes by pointing a warning finger towards my disturbed childhood. An exculpatory circumstance might be that I was raised a half-orphan. You ofcourse can say that's not so bad, she had at least one parent to take care of her, but believe me it is more complicated than that, because neither of my parents are dead yet. But after they decided to live separate lives there was less than half of each left to me. So if you insist on mathematical correctness, I'd raise my rate of orphanhood to three-quarters.

2 Parents : 2 = 1 Parent

1 Parent : 1 New Partner = $\frac{1}{2}$ Parent

$\frac{1}{2}$ Parent : 1 New Born = $\frac{1}{4}$ Parent

 Combined:

1 Parent - $\frac{1}{2}$ Parent - $\frac{1}{4}$ Parent = $\frac{1}{4}$ Parent

So a $\frac{3}{4}$ orphanage leaves you with $\frac{1}{4}$ of both parents. The way I see it, this is worse, and leads to a higher sense of loneliness than if both of them were dead. I do not wish them to die but:

2 Parents − 2 Parents = 0 Parents

That is an equation one surely suffers from, but it is at least something concrete. An empty space is probably easier to fill than a place where still fractions of something remain, lurking in some dark place where they wait to attack you unaware.

What is most disturbing of this all is that society sanctions this kind of ripping apart of parents and by it says yes to the partitioning of children, from whom in return they again by law of society expect to become normal, whole and self-sustaining members of the same society.

?

That's why I am offender on the rules of society. If I should knock on your door, I will never allow you to let me in. Because I was made a criminal, an outlaw and now I cannot get back in. Because something went wrong with my integration; I am amongst you but will never be able to cooperate. I cannot take you with me on one of my crime sprees but still, be prepared to find me on the WANTED – list.

Besides all of this, or because of it, this is, as always, hard to differentiate, I am still not made to be alone; I just cannot manage to live with people. Thus I decided to transfer my need for attachment onto animals. Because I am not the bossy kind of person, I felt no inclination to own a dog. After I tried guinea-pigs, I found that their disposition does not fit mine. That motionless lying in a cage just reminded me that I too cannot get out. After that I was chosen to have a cat. By a lovely, melodious, slow creature named Cloudy, I was transferred from utter loneliness into compassionate heaven. I do not want to bore you with details, but it is crucial that you understand what she was for me. Imagine that all of a sudden you are presented with a daughter: Without having the pain of giving birth, without the painful obligation of nourishing, of providing a healthy family-environment, but with all the benefits of being a mother and that of having a child. As she grew up she became bit by bit what I could not become. She was beautiful and she new it, but she never was vain. She was curious; she wanted to go out and see the world, having a share in adventures and opportunities. But she new her limits: if she accidentally climbed on a tree, she knew she could not come down, so she waited for me to rescue her. Even if it was cold and raining, she would sit there and know rescuing belonged to my competences. She was able to share responsibilities.

When she fell in love she got restless and disappeared for two days. Without hesitation she threw herself in the swamp of love. When she came back she seemed content and could not sit for days. She was brave enough to give birth and raise her kittens. She never gave a thought about the *raison d'être* of life. Maybe she did not even know the term. We woke up together, we ate together, we took long walks together, we moved together and we cried together. Everything was natural and self-evident. There neither was reasoning nor arguments. We were a closed circle, a complete unbelievable we, in a sense that she was not me but a part of me. That part I always longed to be. All pain was gone out of the world. There was reason to go home, to by food, to stay home on party-demanding Saturday nights. I had accomplished what I thought would be out of my reach: I created mysef a home.

All of this seems to be gone forever. Cloudy was lost. She did not come home one Thursday. After five days I slowly lost all the ease her presence provided me with. The fridge was empty, the flat was a mess, and I could not sleep. I sat on the balcony and light candle after candle so she would have a light to guide her home. I searched all the trees in the vicinity even though it was raining heavily, but she was on none of them. I searched all the basements, gardens bushes. Looked in the nearby river, but if she fell in, she would surely have already floated towards the ocean. I was restless but still I had to stay. Looking towards the sky I frantically hoped that I would be granted one wish: to ever see her face again. And I was afraid, that if she did not come back, I would have to take her place, be everything she was, everything I could bear to be. Anguish always leads me to expect the worst, thus I sprouted out verses, as if she really were gone for good.

Smooth, slow, melodious creature,
Half my soul, all my heart.
In the end ten pounds of delicious flesh

Nicely arranged on a Chinese wedding-buffet.

Who wears your precious hide now?
Have you melted into your hiding place?
Have you unravelled into that light
Your eyes shed for three shining years?

Yearning to recount your white whiskers,
Re-register every sweet heartbeat.
You will never be my purring-pillow ever again.
Darkest, deepest, dreadful despair.

You have vanished into thin air, cleared away.
Etherized, vitrified, resinified, nitrified, ozonized.
Returned to dust or simply turned away.
Forgetting who you were; that you eternally belonged
to me.

I imagine you in a plastic bag - cheap funeral veil.
Rotten cabbage -instead of roses- adorns your bier...
You're out there while the rain is pouring -
Swishing, swimming sound of my mourning.

The bedroom window was your crow's nest,

From there we watched the sun set.

Whispering voiceless secrets

While you hunted ill-fated insects.

Priceless traces of your nozzle on the pane

I cannot bring myself to clear away.

Insufferable yet has to be endured pain

In the eerie emptiness of the frame –

--------that's all that remains--------

But as a woman of action I did not restrain myself to writing fancy poems. I also created a poster. I made 300 copies and began to glue them all over the place. Soon my Cloudy would become the most known face in the whole district, I thought, and surely somebody would see her and bring her home to me.

My cat Cloudy got lost on Thursday
(2010. 05.20).

She is black, her belly
and her paws are white.
If you have seen her,
or know where she is please call:

0173-891 43 403
Thank you!

Let me tell you, there were lots of black and white cats here. I saw many in the course of the past two weeks and the calls continued to come in. I was overwhelmed by the readiness to help. I had never suspected my fellow humans to be so compassionate. In this regard I am already reformed a bit, enlightened by the flow of care complete strangers issued towards me. But the best was yet to come.

One morning I got a call from a kind gentleman, who had seen Cloudy. She was hiding in a bush near the fence of a horse stable. He said she had been there for at least 24 hours. He had seen her several times while his dog was taking him out for a walk. In fact, it was the dog that sniffed her out. Even those servile creatures are capable of compassion, I thought, and rode my bicycle to the location. And low, there she was! I was praising all the gods for giving me reason to live again, for the simple mercy of seeing her face again. Cloudy was so dishevelled, so thin, so crazy looking, with a panicky twitch in the tip of her tail. But it was her, I believed, purring, breathing, loving and belonging to me again. She lay in our bed again; I had to ask permission to crawl under the sheets so I would not disturb her recreational naps. She played with the tangling strains of my hair again. She was everything I never was, again and again and again. This time forever, this time forever.

…...............

After several days the euphoria had ceased a little, I was slowly capable of thoughts that do not mainly touch on Cloudy. I bought an enormous bouquet of flowers and a bottle of finest Irish whiskey as a present for the kind gentleman who had made me so happy without demanding anything in return. Before setting out to catch him somewhere on his dog walking round, I decided to snuggle with Cloudy a little bit more. She was as loving as ever, purring and cuddly. Then she climbed upon my legs and well, how should I describe it, she began to make awkward motions, rubbing her belly against my leg in a very explicit way, in a way a she-cat would never do, well, as far as I know. But nowadays everything seems to be possible. Thus I thought this was merely a new habit of hers but then she rolled over on her back. And there it was, pink and unmistakable: a willie, a cock, a penis. In my bed.

The roof of my home collapsed; I was sitting amongst the rubbish considering the feasibility of spontaneous sex-change according to stress and malnutrition. How many quarters of probability? 1:1.000.000? Less? More? With the settling of dust my mind became clearer too.

That's the reason why an incisor was missing and why I was not able to find the scars of a previous accident on her hind-legs. Finally my regressed senses began to work again. In league with my acute mind I drew the conclusion: This cat was not my cat. He was an impostor, a fake, and I was so deluded by my hearts wishes that I was unable to see what was before my eyes. I was deceived, after all my experiences, after all the caution, all the careful preparation of never forgetting that the world is even uglier than it seems. And there was no one to blame. I was sitting here crying my eyes out watching this golem stuffing his belly with the most expensive cat food I had bought for Cloudy, and I was trying to convince my mind's eye to see what the eye in the flesh sees.

Hours went by. I saw the flowers of gratefulness wither; the bottle of Whiskey remained unchanged. The sun moved on its everlasting path, pulling in her wake the Moon, the stars, on one of which my Cloudy now surely resides. I curled up in my sheets, I fell asleep, I dreamt.

I dreamt that I woke up in the morning; I grabbed those almost dead flowers and the bottle. I did not wash, I did not shave, I did not even brush my teeth. I stumbled out of the flat, in my nighties, blindly stumbled to the place where I had found Fake. There he stood, the wise gentleman, holding his attentive dog on a leash.

"You have been crying?"

"How do you know?"

"I am an optician, I should know..."

"Oh, you're just the kind of person I need. You see, I've got this eye-related problems a can hardly bear to see..."

And I told him everything. There was no sound of speech, my eyes were telling him. He could see the doubt and fear of the years gone by, the anguish with which I tried to preserve myself, and the hard fight I had put up against this world. He could see my mathematical struggles to find a definition of me, to finally know something for real and they mildly amused him. He could see the scars of the battles, the pus-filled and unhealed wounds but they did not disgust him. I could close my eyes and he was still able to see me, my depths, my soul, my fluttering heart, barely drumming its usual beat. He saw and he did not care, he wanted, he wanted to have me.

And then I felt, I felt him touching me. I allowed him to, but I wanted to run away. I was so afraid of letting down my guard to finally put my swords away. But then Cloudy came and helped me one last time. His soft hands reminded me of her paws, how she used to touch my face. I did not care to open my eyes, I knew she was with me, she was licking my cheek while she looked me in the eye and told me, unmistakably, I could hear every word: "You may watch me die." And I promised him: "I will."

The Impossible Potato Salad

Maja was studying Biology in Stockholm. Because she originally came from the small village of Mora in Mid-Sweden, she was living in a dorm in the beautiful district of Liljehomen. Opposed to the wide-spread assumption students do not only live for their studies, not even in Stockholm, they frequently (Not often, mind you, not often!) gather together for dancing and a little bit (Mind you again, a little bit!) of drinking. Some of the students try to cover the general purposelessness of these "parties" by giving them a motto, like for example a costume-party. Such a sophisticated bunch of pretenders (A not so wide-spread synonym for students in certain circles.) had invited Maja in her first semester to a vegetable-party.

Maja was a country bumpkin but she painstakingly avoided appearing as one, so she really had to carefully consider her choice of vegetable for the upcoming event. Would a strawberry represent her sweetness or just make her easy prey? Would a carrot be a threat to eventual candidates for dancing or just represent her down-to-earth entrenchedness? If she went as a cabbage, would they just wait for her leaves to fall or would they get her point that they merely represent her ability to unfold only if presented with excellent conditions? To put it simply: she was dithering. She went to the local market, wandered between the stands, and all of a sudden (What is by degrees if this is all of a sudden?) she had it! She will deceive everybody! Understatement is called for! She will go as a potato! Let them wrack their brains over this!

Now that the decision was made, creation had to be done. This was a comparatively easy task. She fabricated a stunning life-like costume with the only exception that it was almost as big as she was. It had the color, the texture and even the bumps every ordinary potato is supposed to have.

On the day of the party, as she was getting ready, she was immensely satisfied with herself and was looking forward to spend a wonderful evening with her vegetable friends.

But, oh, low! There must have been some kind of misunderstanding because she was the only vegetable present! And at that a real huge one! Everybody else was clad as princesses, pirates and all the usual stuff.

Maja, little bumpkin, she still had to learn that costume-parties were much like life: they depend on interpretation. Even pirates eat vegetables if all the rum is gone (and the meat). Maja was rapidly becoming desperate. How could she hide? Where should she go? But life is also based on the principle of Ying and Yang, so there was also relief in store for Maja. After a ring of the doorbell a lovely lettuce-leaf appeared in the room. They instantly bonded.

Dancing was not that easy considering their different dimensions. But after a little bit of bumping, tossing and turning, they managed to melt into one harmonious motion. All the other guests went green with envy eyeing them. Maja could have thought with vengeance that at least now they began to resemble vegetables, but she had other things on her mind... Her lovely lettuce was signaling to her that they should retreat to somewhere more private. When they were happily secluded in one of the bedrooms, they started to open one and other. She could hardly wait to get to the core of this lettuce! Then the inevitable surfaced. Oh, no the lettuce was a girl too! And Maja, our little bumpkin, was not a lesbian.

If Policemen Had Heartaches

If policemen had heartaches,
they would not bark
at innocent people
running against cars
that are polluting the air,
we all are trying to breathe.

If they had heartaches,
their dogs would smell
the loneliness of people
standing in the crowd,
where babies scream,
and birds cry oily tears.

If policemen had heartaches,
they would have seen you
–   revolution's glory and
        the stone in your hand –
like I have; the day
you were begging me to stay.

Désiré Arnold

So Sensual

In the kitchen we are
The water is slowly flowing in the sink
The apple trees outside are in full bloom
You are standing behind me
Caressing my neck
We are looking thru the window
What do we see
The other world besides you and me
The red cardinals hatching
The rain pouring down
Noises from down under the shelter
A cutie called coon
A lick
A bite
A scratch
Our coffee seems to be ready
And I wonder why you undressed me
In the kitchen
For breakfast

Nearby A River

I feel the wetness creeping up my legs
I feel a shiver creeping up my legs
Nearby a river I sit
Nearby that river we met
In rays of daylight
In beams of eyelight
Now it is dark
Only the single standing street lamps
Casting redorange lights onto the water
A duck flying up the tree
A bug sitting on the grass next to me
I empty a bottle in one shot
A stranger asking me where to go
How shall I know
I cannot move
I cannot foresee
Frozenly I am stuck on the bottom
Of a nightmare so endlessly
Run, run, run, the fairy whispered
But I can hardly hear

Erotic Things

Green leaves dancing
           on a tree
A white foaming wave
           breaking on the shore
A cherry hanging on a tree
           I pass by
An open window where the wind
           is flowing in
A red scarf on the neck of a beautiful
           woman
The moving hands of two
           dancers on the stage
The grey rock unmovable and exposed
           to any kind of weather
A dandelion ready to change
           into a Pusteblume to fly
The azur blue sky turning into
           darkblue to meet the stars at night
The orange glooming sun hitting the horizon
           where my eyes meet yours

If....

If Jesus met a prostitute
What would he lo(o)se
Forbidden desires
Of crying priests in vain
Forbidden claims
Of dying tears in rain

If Jesus met a prostitute
What would he lo(o)se
His lust, his heart, his soul
The sensuality of his hands floating over
Cottonlike skin
His temper, his blood, his heat
The sensuality of a mind meeting another
Even-handed mind

If Jesus met a prostitute
What would he lo(o)se
In her
Dreams and screams
For love and approval

Of being someone

In her

Wishes and relishes

For a home

To settle in

If Jesus met a prostitute

Why would it matter

That she used to be a prostitute

Prelude to Macbeth

Scene 1

An open place. Darkness. Rain.

Enter Lady Macbeth, 3 witches.

1 Witch:	You called upon us to meet
2 Witch:	You called ice and fre to calm down your inner longings and desire
3 Witch:	No need to tell what you wish to spell
Lady M:	May I be assured of your assistance?
1 Witch:	Indeed, just stay with us until this full moon is covered by a shade
2 Witch:	Just stay with us until this circle around you is on flame
3 Witch:	Just stay with us until our cries will be shadowed by steam of ice.

Witches vanish.

Lady M: I cannot see. I am blinded by thee.
               What have I done. What have you
               done to me.

Scene 2
Same place. Darkness. Rain. Enter Lady Macbeth. In
tears, on her knees.

Lady M: I cannot sleep. What had led me to
               this deed. My love so pure, my love so
               deep. For this man who seems to
               ignore that he asked my
               father for my hand. For this man who
               seems to deny the man in him, the
               woman in me. For how I wished to
               get a gentle touch. For how I wished
               to find a tender smile. From his heart,
               on his face. But hurt and wounding,
               blood and sweat on steel and metal,
               men on horses riding through the
               night, from fight to fight, from broi to

broil. That's where he puts his heart and mind. Blinded by rage and anger. He sees through me. My heart is not made out of steel and metal. My mind does not smell like mens blood and sweat.I could only beg- please use your sword on me, run it into me, drink from my wounds, nourish yourself from my hurt. But even then- he looked through me.

Scene 3

A heath. Thunder and lightning. Enter three witches.

1 Witch:	What bringst thou?
2 Witch:	The hair we need from him.
3 Witch:	The blood we need from her.
All:	We shall begin when this fire is burnt out. We shall begin as we know what this is all about. Pour down the darkest rain

this night.

Pour down the worms of Eden.

Put shades of mist over any
light.

Where there is blood there
can be no freedom.

Free these souls from laws
and moralities.

Free these souls from
heavens claws and devils
penalties.

Here we stand and see what
humankind can be.

On this earth no sun will be
seen.

On this earth no dew drop
will glance.

Until fulfilled what had to be
fulfilled.

Until done what had to be
done.

Draw blood and evil over
this country.

Let the pure and wise be
unspoken.
This is our will.

Scene 4

An open place. Men on horses. Noises of fght.
Enter Macbeth.

Macbeth: I should be king. No doubts.
              No doubts that this is what
              I wish.
              No doubts that this is what
              I deserve. I fought them
              all, risked my life for this
              land, for my people. I have
              done it all. Yet brave and
              keen I stood, with this
              sword and knife. Not a
              single feeling in my heart but pride.
              Come, revolt, come to me.
              I hunger for more.
              I thirst for thee.
              But wait- what does it help,

what does it do to me?

A deed much greater than

this war.

In my soul a need much

stronger than this fight can

give.

What shall I do to me?

Macbeth vanishes.

Enter Banquo.

Banquo: How I wish this would come

to an end.

How I wish the sun would

shine on that hopeless

horizon.

That all this revolted mist

would turn into a bright new

morrow where we can hear the

laughters of children again,

and smell the blossoming

of flowers instead of the

smell of death and rotteness

from every corner.

Exit.

A Different Perspective

What shall I say, what is there to sayabout that all
You know about it. What do you think I could tell you
more

Yes, of course, I couldBut would it matter
would it change
anything for you
anything for me
anything for him

No, what's done is done
And here I am... a sleep walking ghost
unable to find rest
unable to sleep in silence
unable to be

What's done is done
I didn't think it was wrong
I wanted him, I desired him
So hopelessly
So mindlessly

That I wanted to give my soul
That I wanted to give my all
My past, my now, my future

Yes, of course, I couldBut would it matter
I am dead, and so is he
Never seen him again, not there, not here
Wherever his soul was sent
mine is not supposed to spend
any second with him

To talk it all over again

If I had known,
If I had had that in my mind,
I might have ran away
But there was nothing to lose

I gave him myself
I gave him my all

But he went on walking through our life, yes our life
in blindness

mindless

of anything that was not within him

and as much as I wished to be part of him

he did not let me in

This letter....

written words on paper

a sign of affection, a sign of love

what a fool I was

thinking we could have anything that would bond us

thinking any support would do

to create a common memory

we had so few

Nowadays you say,

we drifted apart

battlefields, wars, swords, fighting

that was all

what was in his mind

that was all

what was in his heart

lusting

desiring

another sword

another bloody body to stab it in

Nowadays you say,

we drifted apart

I stayed at home

isolated in our

castle with moat

and the moat dried out

how I missed him

his face

his eyes

his arms

how I missed him

that line in him

must have dried out

We've been two rivers

mingling

where the white oaks grow

where the fish jump high

where the water keeps boiling

but do I remember

did he ever heat

did he ever retreat

into me

This letter....

now I know

what false face

must hide what false heart

doth know

the deed confounds us

the deed will make us mad

Confound you

Our hands were of the same colour

I reached you mine

you gladly took them

but stayed the blind

No word left your lips

to comfort me

no word left your lips

to console me

You, you, you

inward heart, inward eye

but where, my lord, where was I

I stayed locked up
in your tower
at hand when you needed me the most
at hand when you pleaded against the ghost

My hope was drunk
with isolation, rejection and despair
fair is foul and foul is fair
my ship has sunk

My heart went white
my lips went pale
nowadays you say,
we drifted apart
But I tried
and I tried
and I tried
to be for you
what you wanted me to

The greatest gift between two

I laid to your feet

in the dust, and indeed

you stumbled

you stumbled

who that had a heart to love

help me hence

Mistakenly

I hoped for you

I hoped for your open eyes

But even then,

when my worldly sanity was gone

and all this torture here had begun

all you could think of, my lord,

was you, you ,you

Why did you never care

about me

about us

about our baby

Straight-faced you let me talk anything

did you ever listen

did you ever listen to what I said

Your desire and lust
strong and powerful
you kept it up right
til the end
the climax of your world
that did not bend
Do you know how it feels
do you know what has been in me
so full of passion
so full of love
I didn't ask for anything
I didn't beg for more

You used me
you took out everything from me
by destruction dwell in doubtful joy
why, what care I
for your own good
all causes shall give away

I tried to wash my hands

I tried to burn it all away

darkness scared me

loneliness my only friend

give sorrow words, the grief,

that does not speak

whispers the o'er-fraught heart,

and bids it break

your eyes were open

but your senes were shut

We could have made it

but nowadays they say,

we drifted apart

The queen, my lord, is dead

she should have died hereafter

great words

a tale told by an idiot

I guess you mean me

full of sound and fury,

passion and love, my lord,

signifying nothing....

Signifying nothing

that's what it all meant to you

what shall I say, what is there to sayabout that all.

Yes, of course, I couldBut would it matter

would it change

anything for you

anything for me

anything for him

No, what's done is done

And here I am... a sleep walking ghost

unable to find rest

unable to sleep in silence

still unable to be

We've been two rivers

mingling

and now

it's time to part

to let myself rest

in peace

alone

My soul so rubbed in dust
by you
My heart so white and pale
by you

How I wish
we could undo

Josta van Bockxmeer

Anna Blume Eats a Lot

He had thrown me up in the sky, and broken me down in pieces. I left the house while he was still sleeping. I couldn't resist to pick up some of the empty beer bottles standing around and drop them off next to the nearest carbage can, for the lucky finder. The city was buzzing with people rushing in and out of tubes in the sheer morning light. I crossed the passage underneath the Schönhauser Allee station, drifting through the crowd and being pushed back and forth. I was feeling light and blue and transparent. At the other side of the street was a shopping center. I entered H&M, headed for the fitting room and closed the curtain behind me. The mirror showed an alarmingly normal face, only a bit pale and with dark circles under the eyes. I took off my coat, pullover and t-shirt. The skin underneath was showing black welts all over the back and on the sides. They didn't look like me, I touched them and it hurt. I put on my clothes again and sat down on the floor. I've always liked my body. I remember looking in the mirror in my early teenage years and being satisfied with what I saw. What a different picture now. Why he wounded me I don't know. Maybe he was drunk, at least that's what he said when he saw what he had done. I hate it when grown-up people need excuses like that. When I told him so, he had already fallen asleep. I didn't know if I was feeling sad. It was more as if all motivation had been beaten out of me, so I could not sincerely feel anything anymore. After I had sat in the fitting room for a while it started to be more crowded in the shop, more and more feet appeared from under the curtain. I got up and left the cabin. I went to the shelf with accessories and picked a pair of long, black earrings. On the way to the register I stumbled, stepped on somebodies toes and threw over a stand with hats. Stupid things happen at the unhappiest moments. The earrings made me feel heavier, as if they gave me something to hold on to. Outside I headed for the tube station. On the stairs to the platform there was a concert by a violin, a didgeridoo, and a djembe, which gave me a reason to linger for a while. The smell of urine was terrible, but the rhythm made me drift away from the city into a strange but relieving sphere. I started to feel hungry.

Close to Eberswalder Straße is a cheerful and relatively quiet breakfast place called Anna Blume. It is a little bit expensive, but the presence of young, artistic and wealthy Wahlberliner made me feel good. They are the kind of people that you see taking place in a coffee bar in the early afternoon, leaning back, breathing in the odour of the city and saying: "I'm so happy to be here!" Despite everything that happened I was still here, I told myself. Being able to sit in this bar was an achievement for itself, the rest would come later. A young mother, dressed in skinny jeans and a big coloured shirt, was trying to teach her three-year-old how to eat a bagel with avocadocream and cottage cheese with fork and knife. The little one only seemed to show interest in the bread and the sugar canes that came with dad's coffee. Dad was sitting on the side of the table, hidden behind his laptop and did not notice the disappearance of his sugar. On the large sofa two girls, perfectly beautiful girls without any visible welts, were sipping café latte and nibbling from a fruit salad. I would need something heavier. The waiter came and I ordered a café latte and the big mediterranean breakfast, plus some extra scrambelled eggs and a piece of chocolate cake. For a moment I thought he would ask: „Are you sure you can pay for that?" But he just wrote down my order and nodded friendly. The parts of me that were not covered by my clothes seemed to look quite normal. Or maybe it was the attitude of the Berliners, who wouldn't even be surprised if I would have been sitting here in a pink rabbit suit. With every bite I felt more sick and lightheaded. After the meal I staggered upon the street.

There are days on which people give way to me in the streets as if it's the most natural thing to do. I don't even have to ask, my appearance is strong enough to get my own space immediately. This day was definitely not like that. Despite of all the food I ate and the feeling of being big that came with it I kept on having to step aside, even though the sidewalk was broad and almost empty. A father with one of these large, red, modern buggies with large wheels came around the corner and immediately bumped into me. Without saying a word he walked on, as if he hadn't even seen me. Furiousness rose up from my stomach, but I was feeling too light in the head and too heavy from the food to give expression to that feeling. I walked for a while without really knowing where to go and ended up at Schönhauser Allee again. I sat down at the side of the passage underneath the station, leaning against the green balustrade. The strange thing about your environment is that you never see your own presence. The whole world is there, the trees, the cars, the blue signs of the tube stations, the tomatoes being sold at the grocery shop, the children, the business people, and most of all the mothers and fathers with their children. Only the place where I am standing is an empty spot. If other people don't see me like the man with the buggy, then do I still exist? The nice thing about not existing is that you don't have to decide where to go next. I could just let myself drift on whatever stream would come, nobody would be disturbed by me, and I wouldn't have to worry about what would happen. I could for example just follow that man collecting empty beer bottles over there, to see what he was doing in his life. He must have been already over fifty years old, since his grey hair was turning white at his temples. The back of his head was showing a thick, fatty dreadlock, of the kind that really is the result of not combing your hair for years. He was pushing a shopping cart full of colourful bottles. When he crossed the road I followed him on a distance. He was walking slowly and constantly looking around him, from time to time reaching for some bottles next to trashcans. He entered the Mauerpark from the north side, parked his cart next to a lamp-post and walked unto the grass. Then he started to collect all the bottles that were lying around in little heaps, the left-overs from the party last night. I sat down on the grass and pretented to be busy looking at the horizon. After a while, his cart was chockfull by now, he went on.

The closest supermarket was Rewe in the Kulturbrauerei, which is quite far to walk with such a full cart. It was bumping on the uneven pavement and from time to time a bottle would fall off. One glass bottle broke. He seemed to have trouble picking them up all the time, maybe he had a sour back. At Rewe the security man greeted him shortly but in a friendly way. I waited a few seconds before following him into the shop, pretending to read a poster which announced an offer for cheap beef. Inside I found him at the reverse vending machine, concentratingly putting the bottles in one by one. It took him at least twenty minutes, and behind him the queue was growing; and annoyed prenzlauer bergers started to couch and shuffle with their feet. I wondered how well he could live from collecting bottles. The cart contained at least 100 of them. 100 beer bottles are eight euros, and then there are the PET-bottles, of which he had collected many more, and which bring 25 cents per piece. Say he would need three hours to collect 100 of them, that would still make a pay of eight euros an hour. When he was done the longest deposit bottle receipt I had ever seen came out of the machine. He turned it in at the register and received the money, went out and parked his shopping cart behind a döner shop. Then he walked to the station Eberswalder Straße and entered the tube. I did the same, but I got in through the next door and stood about five meters apart from him. It was one of these old-fashioned tubes with the narrow benches on the side, in which the people sit opposite of each other and the rest has to stand in between. I was standing in the middle in the very crowded wagon, trying to hold myself upright. The bottle collector had found himself a better spot next to the door, where he could lean against the board at the side of the bench. He got out at Alexanderplatz, and while walking through the corridors of the station he still picked up some bottles here and there. Maybe it had become a habit which he couldn't control anymore, some kind of an occupational disease. He entered the U8 and I took the next door again. This time it was rather empty, so I was able to sit. The bottle collector was standing at the door again. As we departed the station Heinrich Heine Strasse, we heard a voice from the back "Tickets please!" The second ticket-inspector came from the other side. I was a bit panicked, because I had forgotten to buy a ticket. The bottle collector got checked first. He didn't have one either, but took a street paper from his bag, and the inspector left him in peace. As he checked the ticket of the woman next to me an then turned in my direction, I felt nerves come up in my throat. But strangely enough he didn't ask me and went to the girl on my other side. First I was wondering about my luck, but then I remembered that I was probably still non-existing, I had almost forgotten about it.

The bottle collector got out at Kottbusser Tor and

took the exit in the direction of Kaisers. Inside the supermarket he first returned the bottles, then made a round through the shop. To my surprise I saw him buying some delicious food, ciabatta bread, smoked salmon, cucumber, avocado, tomato and lemon. He payed with the receipt from the machine, greeted the girl behind the register and walked out. Outside he approached a group of men and one woman who were sitting on the ground and drinking beer, some of them were holding a pack of the street paper „Motz". They patted him on the back and talked to him, gave him a beer and they toasted. He put the food in the middle of the group and got a round of applaus. They started to eat, there was a lot of laughing and talking. I sat down a little distance apart and waited. One of the dogs of the group had been looking at me with a somehow very sincere expression on his face, and now came walking towards me. He sniffled and I stroke his head. One of the men looked and said "He, Ronja has found a new friend!" The bottle collector looked too, stood up and walked towards me. He seemed very tall while he was standing and I was sitting, but his face was friendly. He said "He, I think I saw you in the subway already. What are you doing here?" "I don't know, I had nowhere to go and then decided to follow you." I was too tired to lie. He didn't seem to mind. "Do you want to eat with us? It is my birthday" I nodded and got up, walked with the dog and the man towards the group. They made me some space and gave me some food. "What is your name?" the bottle collector asked. "Anna Blume", I said and with every bite I felt myself getting heavier.

Woordeloos

als jij - en als ik
en ik jou – en jij mij
und wenn wir
-nein, das ist zuviel gesagt
mit andern worten
also das gleiche - aber nicht
nur ich dich - und du mich
yes we
not too much
the same - in different
I mean - do you see
ja ik zie het - voor ogen
want als ik jou en jij mij
weisst du
was ich meine

Sprachverwirrung

(to)taalverwarring, total confusion
too much said teveel gezegt
words scattering breaking
against the wall
but the meaning is still drifting
het daalt niet neer
op het papier es schwebt
vor meinen Augen ungreifbar
unbegreiflich onbegrijpelijk
geballte Fäuste uttering frustration
zu viel gesagt teveel gezegd
aber zwischen den Worten
bleibt es still

Regine Glaß

Lisa

Marcus was playing with Frank on a sunny afternoon.
He thought: „What a perfect day! Waking up to the
sound of birds. Having cake for breakfast, because
yesterday it was the birthday of our little sister, Lisa.
Altough Lisa is the big, fat problem in our life, to eat her
birthday cake isn't much of a problem. Lisa always wants
to play with us! Doesn't she realise that she is 5 years
old and a girl? Doesn't she realise that we are already 9
years old and boys? She is supposed to go into her
room to play with dolls, instead of trying to talk to us!"
Marcus and Frank were playing their favorite game.
They were hanging out of the window, trying to spit on
the heads of the people who passed by. Suddenly Lisa
went into the room.
„What are you doing here?" she asked with her
annoying, high, girly voice.
„We are just enjoying the nice weather!", Marcus tried
to sound as innocent as possible. He knew, that if Lisa
realized what they were doing, she would go and tell
everything to their mother.
But they didn't count on the mature brain of their

sister, who thought in this moment:

„I have already seen, what the boys have done! Wow, this seems to be very exciting! I just want to take part! To be part of the gang! I know, that the boys think that playing with little girls is boring. Of course, because I am not interested in playing with little girls, either! All this talking about dolls, horses, butterflies and princesses! What a pity! I want to provoke! I want to be bad and exciting! I want to spit on the heads of people walking by and to fight a battle, pretending that I am a cowboy!" But Lisa wasn't supposed to be part of the gang. She looked down to her pink skirt, which her mother was so proud to be able to buy for her. And realized, that she would never be part of the gang.

Underneath the window, a young lady passed by. She looked very studiousus and was wearing jeans and a black bagpack. Suddenly she looked up to the window, where the three of them were standing. First, she looked a bit annoyed, then she was smiling at Lisa, waving at her and took her way alone in the street. Lisa knew now, that she would fight her battle. Maybe with a bagback, maybe in jeans. But surely alone, but never lonely.

The Prayer

 Michael is sitting in his train to work. This Morning he
had the idea to listen on the way to work just to songs
from 2007, so he had updated his i-pod with records
from Arcade Fire, Shout out Louds and Bloc Party.
He is just listening to "The Prayer" by Bloc Party, which
was his favorite dancefloor song, back in these old days,
when he was still going to university in this seaside
town, where everyday was like sunday. While
remembering this town with these words, he laughed
out loud. Two years ago,he left university and he seems
to be still this indie-rock student who even thinks in
the words of Morrissey.So, 10 minutes left, time for my
daily exercise, he tinks. He stretches his leg,he moves
his feet, still these driving lines in his ears."Lord give me
grace, and dancing feet."
And now the other one.
"Stop! What am I doing here?"
The question crashes into his mind, so fast that he isn't
able to say if it comes from his brain, his heart or even
his feet. Suddenly, this exercise, that he practises
everyday in the last 10 minutes of his ride to work,

seems that ridiculous to him."

"When did that happen to me? When did I became such a conformist that the only movements in my life are taken with my toes while I am sitting?"

And while the next movement is happening, Michael is absolutly sure, that the instruction comes from is heart with a little help from his brain. He starts to dance. From this seat, in the first class, some side-steps to the toilet, some pirouettes in the bike-area, some crafty jumps up- and downstairs and a melodious silly walk through the door to the second class, where his eyes meet the eyes of a girl, who was listening to music, sitting with a thoughtful and earnest look, staring out of the window.

The next instruction comes strictly from his heart. No brain is involved. He takes the hand of the girl as she sits there, so beautiful in grey, with hair coloured red. He twists her in small, living circles, while the train is still running the way he runs everyday.

Here it stops. Here is Michaels corporation, here is his firm, here is is office.

The next instruction comes from his brain. No heart is involved. He goes out of the train. He steps into the

122

office. He smiles in a shallow way, when his eyes meet the eyes of some collegue. He turns on his computer and starts to work.

The incident on the train did never happen, he says to himself.

He does a good job today. While he is packing his stuff to go home, the collegue who works next to him asked:

"Would you mind to have some afterwork-drink with me? They have a very good bourbon in the bar on the other side of the street?"

"Of course, I'd love to", Michael answers. They talk about work and strange incidents on the train, which seem to happen every day.

"What a strange city!", Michael laughs, leans back and orders another glass of bourbon.

Turned into Sitcom Dialog

 Your table. A cup of coffee. A cigarette, just taken from a brand new package. The TV in front of us. The coffee is black, of course, because you never go shopping on saturdays. I never expected you to remember that I drink my coffee in a girly manner with milk and sugar.

I've expected you to stay awake with me from friday 'til saturday. Watching one season of Scrubs. Laughing, glad to know that we don't have to talk, ignoring the fact, that we actually enjoy each others company, just sitting around and doing some meaningless stuff.

I've expected you to have no plans for the rest of the weekend except sleeping, waiting until the sun disappears again and you finally dare to go to the chinese restaurant on the other side of your street to buy some take-away duck and another package of cigarettes from the store right beneath your flat. Smoking, until you fall asleep again. Waking up early in the sunday morning, in fear that you might had set yourself on fire.

I've expected you to pretend, that you just liked this

well-working way of life and you couldn't wait until I go.
Me, disturbing you in your lonesomeness, practiced for
two   years   now.
I've   expected   you   to   be   funny.
I've expected us to keep silence about the way we
recognize each other in our twenty-something-like pain.
I've expected us to turn our conversations into sitcom
dialog.
I've expected you too ask me about 4'o clock in the
afternoon if I had any plans for the rest of the weekend
and of course you were expecting me to admit: "Sure.
At 8 o'clock, I'm gonna meet some friends in a bar. So I
have   to   go   now."
Staring at your pale-blue eyes, which could, cut from
your face, be my own pale-blue eyes, while having some
kind of deja-vu, taking another cigarette from the
package, I am not allowing myself to ask, what could
happen if I am going to stay one single saturday evening.

126

Girl Disguised as a Squirrel

The girl disguised as a squirrel
is loosing fur, again.
She wears a suit
with a big, funny tail
She thinks of blood,
she thinks of love,
and runs against her frightening past.
The girl who became a squirrel
isn't able to talk, anymore.
She became part of the nature,
of the silence and the spirit
of the wood.
But the tiger inside of her left.

Things and -ships

Time: 22:15, Friday Evening, October.
Place: Some Bar in Neukölln, One small Room, an audience of Hipsters and old frequenters.
A lady comes into the room. She could be young, she could be old. It doesn't make a difference. What matters is the fact, that she looks a bit drunk and there is a cheap guitar in her hand. She takes a step to the stage, then she stumbles until she finally sits down.

With strong Voice:

,,My idea grew in a chat with a friend. To call it a chat, is a big understatement, to make it quite clear. To call him a friend is a big understatement, to make it quite clear. I come to the point:

If human beings just happen to function like machines, they become objects.

So, most people just wish to function in every minute, in every feeling, in every second, in every circumstance.

(She takes out a big box)

If I turned all the heavy feelings I've felt and the persons who were more ore less responsible for that into objects, they would fit into my box, after my singing is finished.

Sit down here, friends, just take a glass of wine and watch, what will be thrown away into my box.

I The Flag

I met you at the dirtiest pub.
I was drunk as hell.
We talked about politics and music and films,
I guess.
I don't really remember
you were a revolution for me.
You killed me young, innocent
and convinced of the good.

II The Computer

Help me while I am sleeping,

type your code and I will dream.

Give me safety and anti-virus scans.

I'll give you input

and type my words.

You don't understand but work out.

III The Dancing Shoe

The music is loud

we shake our heads.

Your eyes meet mine.

You're a really pretty guy, dude!

We are dancing, we are drinking.

I'll take you home.

We have this night

and I'd like to see you

never again!

IV The Book

You can read my thoughts

I will turn the page.

If I'm close, you're far away

If I go, you scream.
I turn around and stay
and you go ahead in silence.
I'm alone in the library
of broken dreams and desperation.

V The Light

Always searching for the light.
You were drinking,
I was dancing.
Then we started our fight:
We get prisoned.
And I never wanted to stop
dancing
in the police disco light.

VI The Picture

It's the colours you love
and the words you adore.
It's my body you stroke
and my mind you break through.

When I leave you, you cry
If I'd stay it 'll be worse.
Art is in the eye of the beholder
I don't like to exhibit myself.

VII The Bridge

To stand somewhere where wind lives
and the smell of water is overwhelming.
We meet at the turning points of our life
I'm suffering from toothache.
Beneath all these -ships
we cannot exist.
Except in undefined waves of fresh nothing."

Nobody dares to clap his hands or even to laugh. There
is silence in the room. The Lady has a proud smile. She
takes her guitar, stumbles for the last time, says
„Goodbye, have a nice evening, everybody!" in a sweet
voice and leaves the room.

Wood

"It's that crazy! I've lost my key, again!" Joanna cried and kicked angrily at her bike. It was last week, she lost the key to her bike, had to break her own lock, looking like a thief. Why was this happening now, while she was walking around in the rain on the other side of the town. It had to be there! What was she doing here anyway? She already had known, that it is absolutley meaningless to talk to him; it would be the same everytime they were together! He didn't change at all. Her brain did understand, but her heart stucked in some way. What was this? She found something in the inside pocket of her bag. It felt so soft and so natural on the one hand, on the other so rough and tough. Was it some kind of wood? How was it put into her bag? "Oh!", she laughed as she recognized that it was one of the expensive cigarillos she stole with Peter last summer from her father's house. They walked a long way from home then, to find the right place at the river to sit down, smoke and talk about utopian things.

But summer was gone now, the river was nearly frozen, since November came with its cold and hard spirit, which carries all your hopes and wishes for the future in the backyard of your life. But it's always good to smoke when you're feeling like shit. Her hands were so cold, when she took out the lighter and lighted the last cigarillo. She leaned against the wall of her ex-boyfriend's house. Wasn't that ironic? It was no option to go into the house again. She had to go home by train and come back tomorrow to brake the brand new lock again. FUCK! Imagining herself in summer, smoking with Peter, it was hard for her not to think of the photos he had taken of her. Her full face, her profile, a view of her hand, holding the cigarillo. Wearing a white top. He always liked her dressed in white. And her chain of white pearls, which was from her grandmother. He liked to call her "Girl Anachronism" because he thought she was more like a Hollywood-lady from the fifties than a postmodern girl. Wow, so many things, he said, she was, she acts, she wanted...

All the things he said while they were smoking on expensive cigarillos. The made her forget, how she defined herself. All the photos he had taken, they made her forget how she looked. His camera became her mirror. Now she was smoking alone. And she recognized: She was a girl, who lost the keys to the lock of her bike very often, who leaned at the wall of her ex-boyfriends house in November and smokes on her father's expensive cigarillos. She looked quite good. Desperation suits every postmodern girl.

Marcus Rehm

A Brother's Confession

My Lord I seek you in this darkest hour, which hath
been orchestrated by my foul gone scheme of uniting
the dreadfully hating families Capulet and Montague. By
no means did I plan such a vile outcome on purpose,
yet it was my wrong,
for I should have exercised patience where haste was
present and humbleness should have taken the place
whence plotting has taken the better of me.
Oh my lord I have disappointed you most profoundly.
Sin boarding next to the seven has gripped my soul and
frost hath fallen upon my mind. As much as it pains me I
have to revisit the sights of what has burnt itself into
my head.
The doom of what should have been the noon of a new
family. Being the Lord of forgiveness maybe you will
find it proper to dawn on what is dusk on my soul.

Fate unfolded when this young and zealously eager
youth visited me, to tell me of his newest bve.
Hearing the boy talking about his unrefined emotions
towards a young lady, speaking in the highest tones of
her, I couldn't help myself and smiled. So often this boy

already told me about his latest amour, and in utter honesty my lord, I really couldn't take him seriously anymore. No matter how infatuated he always was, just a couple of months later he already had a new, well…, object of desire. Still I listened to him and gave some council here and there and yet I was partially astounded how this boy replied in a grown up fashion that I wasn't used to. I listened more carefully then and what I heard seemed to be genuine affection reaching deeper than his stories ever did before. Positively surprised, I encouraged him to go seriously about this girl, which seemed to mark a new way of thinking and feeling in this boy. A flash of horror though spilled over me when I finally learned the truth about his adored girl and that she was that young heir of Capulet!

I quickly renounced my advice and warned him about the trouble he would get tangled up in. Of course that boy didn't want to hear any of it and using my words of preached love against me, I had no reason not to trust that boy and his love for Juliet. I should have been more persistent and consistent at this moment and all my sin be washed away, all death been sparred to thee and joy would have taken me.

142

Yet at this instant it immediately dawned on me that this Romeo & Juliet could be the binding remedy that could unite both families for real. Yes my lord, now I know how overwhelmingly foolish I was when I spoke the words of binding, approved their marriage, without the consent of their elders, without even the knowledge of their parents. Even though the purposeful marriage was about to reap its inheritance, the world's keeper enacted his workings against the matters at hand, twisting and coagulating true love and eager desire with a distinctive twist of ill time into a bane of what would be right and proper.

Chosen by the Capulets themselves and with charge invested by infatuation, the young Paris was spurred into eager satisfaction. A marriage arranged to marry the wife again, making her a happy bride and wife to Paris brought woe on the weal of married Juliet.

Deaths within the ranks instilled by Capulet on Montague and vengeance firing back on the aggressor evoked an exiling edict of the prince to this matter. The vindication for Mercutio, murdered by the hands of

Capulet, enraged the hands and dimmed the mind of the newlywed Romeo. Hence this young lad, filled with rage, murdered his way into qualifcation for exile.

Darker the hours grew, as action and reaction drew situations in its wake that needed desperate remake. Time, my lord, was not on our side and so I devised a hasty plan upon an ill decision. Severing Juliet from her ties of future marriage and releasing her from her parents grip, the deception with death would do the trick. This draught concocted with well dosed poison, a remedy to her shackles amongst her kin, will soon give way to love within. This plan though caught up badly, for the letter to Romeo was not delivered. If only I had taken the matter into my own hand, Romeo would have been privy to the plan. How the boy got message of his wife's ending is beyond my intellectual kenning, but it gave birth to suicidal demanding. Here, my brd, is where I truly failed. Here is where the story truly ailed, for what is missing in this situation is a priest with a determined vocation. Where prayer should have guided me, instead the streets cobblestones passed under me. Where fear had taken hold of me, my knowledge of the situation should have resolved the deprivation. Oh my lord I didn't know that this Romeo, driven mad by love, would be desperate enough to end his own living.

Yet too late I was to show him comfort. Too late I was to tutor him. Too late I was to intercept his step.

At the time I regained control and ran back from whence I came the bells already called out in pain and the deaths of the once living I had forsaken were irredeemably lost to my cowardice.
Although the families mourning has brought them closer and therefore Romeo and Juliet's legacy has been unity at last, my failure keeps them from joining in. I will repent my Lord until you have found purpose for cowardice.